B

SIBLINGS

A Twentieth Century Family

SIBLINGS

A Twentieth Century Family

WENDY ROBERTSON

Damselfly Books

COPYRIGHT

SIBLINGS

Wendy Robertson 2022
ISBN: 9798442413076
Imprint: Damselfly Books

DEDICATION

This collection of short stories is dedicated to my mother Barbara and her siblings. Her family of storytellers embedded and embroidered their often-told stories not only into the history of their own family but also significantly into the history of the 20th century.

In the process it seems to me that this habit of storytelling - involving as it does an instinct for the creative power of language and communication - has led in this family, in succeeding generations to success in education to masters and doctoral level and also in some cases to the wider world of publication.

In writing and collecting these stories into a whole underlying narrative I have realised that this instinct to tell stories and then to write them down is a golden inheritance to us all from Barbara and her siblings well into the Twenty First Century.

ACKNOWLEDGEMENTS

I realise now that it takes a village to put together even a small volume such as this. So I would like to offer heartfelt thanks to Avril Joy, Gillian Wales, and Donna Maynard for their valued literary wisdom; to Fiona Naughton for her wonderfully appropriate cover art; and to Anne Dover for her moving narration of these stories which lit up Christmas 2021 for me when they were broadcast on Bishop FM.

WENDY ROBERTSON

CONTENTS

1. BRAM

1922 January 22 British Troops roll over Dublin's cobbled streets and take up positions on the docks and market areas

So. There is this man in our Front Room. Our Dee whispers in my ear that this is a big man from the pit. He's sitting on the horsehair sofa talking to our Mam, his flowing tweed coat unbuttoned and his white silk muffler tight around his neck.

Our Mam is sitting on the music stool in front of the harmonium on which, each night after we've gone to bed, she practices for the Sunday services. She plays in our own chapel on Sunday mornings and at the Welsh chapel at Chilton at the evening service. She makes us go to the services at our own chapel but we don't have to bother with the Welsh chapel, where the words are all jumbled up. It's not jumbled for Mam, of course – her being proper Welsh. Our Eirwen does go there, as she always clings to Mam and is a bit daft that way. But at least she gets to speak a bit of Welsh so that's probably a good thing.

Anyway, here now in our Front Room is this big man in the big coat. We're all here, even though we're never normally allowed in the Front Room. Mostly we're just in the kitchen and the scullery. The Front Room is for best.

But now, here we are - me, Eirwen and our Dee (whose Scottish name is Diordrach), our Aderyn (whose Welsh name

1

means *bird* but round here they call her Ada which means nothing).
We are all sitting on the chairs lined up against the back wall,
Breedlen (whose Welsh name means *helper* but round here they call
her Bridd) and our young Evan, are sitting cross-legged in front of
the fire.

'Well, Mrs. Angus ...' the man's voice sounds like a kind of
whispery roar. 'We know your lad Bram is a good scholar. Your
Jimmy's friends tell us that.'

Mam nods, her eyes wary at the mention of our Da's name.
She sits up straighter on the stool. 'Our Bram passed the School
Leaving Certificate when he was 12 and they let him leave school
then.' She speaks in English but her words swim up and down in
that Welsh way.

The big man crosses his legs and leans back on the horsehair
sofa, which creaks. 'Like I say, a clever lad. They tell me that he's
working in that tailor shop on the High Street?' He raises his
eyebrows.

Mam nods. She's proud of our Bram. 'Yes,' she says. 'He's
apprenticed to the clerk there. Only got the job, look you, because
he's a good scholar.

'Mmm,' He grunts. 'No pay, like?'

'He'll start on a wage on Boxing Day.' Mam's lips close tight
together. Tight.

He strokes his bristly chin. 'That's as mebbe, Mrs Angus.'
He pauses. The ticking of the clock on the mantelpiece is very
loud. Then he coughs. 'Your Jimmy did well down the pit didn't

he? Got to be deb'ty when he was not much more than a lad. That was before he volunteered, like, in fourteen.' He pauses. Then he looks around at us one by one. I shrink back. 'And left you with seven bairns to keep.'

Her eyes, cold as ice now, look him up and down. He glances around our Front Room with the clock on the mantelpiece and the bulky harmonium bought second-hand for her by my Granda so she would play in the services in his Welsh chapel. After my Da died in the war he sent us a bag of pairs of boots left over from his spare time job as a cobbler. All boys' boots of course. Me, I refused to wear them, although our Dee loves hers and wears them when she goes out to play chasey and football with the lads.

Now here in the Front Room the big man coughs and nods his head. 'Well, like, I have instructions from Mr Stevenson to talk to you about all this.'

Bridd's voice tickles my ear. 'Mr Stevenson's *his* big boss at the pit.'

The man's thick fingers stroke his bristly chin again. 'Well, Mrs Angus, it's three years now, isn't it, since we lost Jimmy and all our other lads? And we see even now that Jimmy's a big miss to you as well as the pit.' He pauses and examines his fingernails.' But in these years since the war, haven't you had this colliery house in this fine row?'   He looks again around the bright Front Room 'And of course the coal for your fire.'

A dark cloud settles now around us.

He coughs. 'Well, Mrs Angus, it boils down to this. Mr Stevenson says I should explain that there's talk of new men coming up from Cornwall to fill the gaps left in the workforce by the war. And the houses – only granted to working miners - are needed for their families.'

Mam sighs very loudly and I want to cry. Then she puts her hands together as though she's praying and looks around the room. 'You want us out, then?'

The big man coughs yet again. 'Mebbe that won't quite be necessary, Mrs Angus.' He surveys us, one by one. 'How old is your oldest again? The one that works at the tailor's?'

'Our Bram'll be fourteen next Monday.'

'Well then! There's a solution to your problem. The lad's fit enough to work in the pit isn't he? Then he'll be your working miner. So you can keep your house and your coal. And, being a clever lad, he won't start at the very bottom.' The big man stands up, re-buttons his topcoat and reties his muffler. 'So you'll think about this Mrs Angus?'

She hauls herself to her feet and turns towards the front door. Like the Front Room, it's rarely used. The last time it was used was when an officer in DLI uniform brought the letter from the army to say how brave our Da had been and how the King was proud of him. I was only seven then but I remember it like it was yesterday.

Now the big man shakes Mam's hand and looks her in the eye. 'Come Monday I'll get Tab Smith, who worked marras with your Jimmy, to call here for your lad at half five sharp. Tab'll take him in-bye and make sure he gets to know the ropes from the start.'

Mam tries to pull her hand away, but he clutches it more closely. 'It's the only way, Mrs Angus. It's for the best, you know it and I know it.'

She slams the door behind him and stands with her back to it. Her eyes glittering and her teeth clenched.

We know that look. We begin to melt away through the middle door and make our way through the kitchen, through the scullery and down the backyard. We race out onto the Green behind the houses where Bridd has a store of clay which we can make into beads and buttons to bake them on a tray in the oven.

At 8 o'clock my brother Bram marches down the yard in his shiny black shoes and leaps straight upstairs to hang up his white shirt his jacket and his black trousers. He comes down in bare feet wearing an old shirt and sits at the kitchen table on the end of which Mam has spread a white cloth. Bram sits down and bends his long gangly body over the table, his mop of black hair falling over his eyes. (The rest of my brothers and sisters have shiny black hair like Mam's: all except me, that is. My hair is rusty red like my Da's. My Mam told me once not to worry about that, as the Queen of the Icenae had red hair and she was a brave woman.)

Bram grins across at Aderyn and me, his white teeth flashing. Before him on the table is his meat and potato pie. It was made by Aderyn, who is now Mam's right-hand-woman in the house. She gets to stay off school on Mondays to help Mam with the washing, and on Wednesdays for the ironing and baking.

Bram spears his fork into the crisp golden pastry. Mam stands watching him, her back to the roaring fire, her arms folded. The rest of us – all six of us – are scattered around the room in our nightclothes. Bridd is sitting on a wooden cracket, her hands busy with her knitting needles. Deirdrach is leaning on the windowsill humming a tune. Evan is leaning on the fireguard by Mam's knees. And our Eirwen is staring dreamily out of the window.

Bram grins across at Mam. 'Real good, these taties, Ma. Has Uncle Davey been over?' He wipes his mouth with the back of his hand. At last he notices the silence in the room and turns to cast his eye over each of us. Eventually he looks at Mam and smiles his sweet smile. 'Now, Mam, I was wondering what you're gunna give us for me birthday. Is it a secret?'

She shakes her head, her eyes cold. 'The pit, Bram. Your birthday present is the pit.'

On the Monday following, all of us except Dee are watching for Bram to come home from the pit. Dee is off with some lads down in the woods because her mate Bobby Vann says he's seen these other lads dancing down there. The rest of us hear the sneck on the back gate click and we watch as Bram comes down the yard. His brow and his chin are as black as his hair. His jacket and shirt are grey with coal dust. When he sees us his white teeth gleam in his face.

We are prepared; Bridd has hauled in the tin bath from the yard. Aderyn has filled it with hot water, using the long-handled ladle to dip into the boiler beside the fire. Mam has set the big clothes-horse around the bath and draped sheets over it. For Bram's modesty, like. Evan's job is to be at the ready to scrub his brother's back with soap and the rough flannel. We can hear the boys laughing and talking behind the makeshift screen. Then we watch as Bram's clean shirt and trousers vanish from the clothes-horse. And so, before our eyes, he emerges from his tent, his face shining and clean except for the glamorous black lines around his eyes.

He sits down at the table opposite Mam, who is ladling rabbit stew onto a plate for him. She nods at him her face bland. 'Well son' she says, 'how was the pit then?'

Post Scriptum

So there you are. Our Bram worked down the pit from when he was fourteen until he was sixty two years old. In that time he made good progress up the complicated professional pit ladder. Like our Da Jimmy he became a Deputy at a young age. And in the following years he became a great expert on the intricacy of the seams of coal and the mines that crisscrossed the underworld of County Durham. Interestingly some of the seams and pits have

7

women's names such as Beamish Mary, Ravensworth Betty and Emma. Others have historic names like Ladysmith. Others are named for places like Newton Cap, Princes Street Drift, Throstle Gill and Hole in the Wall.

It all remained poetry to him. The world underground the green surface of our county was his universe. All his life he was driven to talk about this world to whomsoever would listen. Our Bram truly was a good scholar and his university was the pit.

1922. February 16. Unemployment now over one million, including 348,000 ex-servicemen.

2. DIORDRACH

1922. March 8. Allies occupied
Germany to collect war debts.

Our Dee (her given Scottish name *Diordrach* means *pilgrim*, no less!) has always been the scamp of the family. She calls me 'aar kid' and has this crooked smile with a gap between her front teeth. I watch her a lot. She is the oldest girl in our family and the bravest, shown by the fact that she's willing and very able to cross swords with Mam at least once a week. Between them they can convert our kitchen into a war zone. Our Mam - who has everyone else at a word - has never been able to stop our Dee from clumping about after the lads or climbing trees in the boots our Granda sent us from Chilton, to thank for Mam playing the organ in his Welsh chapel.

Our Mam's brother Uncle Job, who brought the boots in a big hessian sack, tumbled them out onto the table like so many leather creatures. Uncle Job fought with our Da in the War, you know. The boots were not new. They were castoffs from our Granda's spare-time job as a cobbler. Our Granda is quite the businessman. As well as being a big man at the Pit and the Chapel he makes and sells tin cooking dishes and has his own billiard hall.

Anyway Dee has always liked to get dirty so the boots come in handy for her Saturday job helping Joe Hunter at his allotment. For pay she brings home potatoes and Brussels sprouts and stuff, so that at least wins her a grim smile from Mam.

And sometimes our Dee tells me her ghost stories. We sit in the backyard with our backs to the end wall and she stretches her long legs out in front of her and clicks her stout heels together. Then she starts off in this fluting voice: not like her voice at all. 'I seen our Granda, Ayla. I seen him in this flapping priest's cloak with his old grey cap on the side of his head.'

'That can't be a ghost, Dee. Our Granda's not dead.' I feel the slack movement of her big shoulders. 'You seen him in Chilton Chapel last Saturday? Didn't you?'

'Aye. I seen him!' She pauses then goes on. 'Right! So he isn't dead, Ayla. I know that. But I saw him down the edge of the woods when he was really at the Pit.' She wriggles her back against the rough stone wall. 'But as well as that I seen Granda's own Da...' She pauses. Quite the drama queen, our Dee. '...and that one's definitely dead, isn't he? Died back there in Wales where they come from. You know! The one that used to sing Welsh songs about marching with Bleddyn ap Cynfyn. I don't know the words of that song, like. Wish I did.'

Then comes the day she creates a real ruckus in the boys' yard at school. Being a girl, she's not even allowed in the boys' yard. Anyway this day she sets two of the lads in her gang on this lad who accused her of being as 'easy as an old blanket'. She even gets in a few kicks herself and manages to split the lad's nose like squashed beetroot,

Anyway this schoolmaster comes to the house - front door again, like the officer - to report the incident to Mam, scolding her like she was a child. One glimpse of him through the middle door and our Dee vanishes through the back door, probably to the den she and her gang have built on the lower reaches of the pit heap.

Then there is the day - it is a Saturday and my brothers are playing football on the green - when this woman comes to the house, sent by the school. Front door again. The woman has her hair pulled back in a big bun and is wearing shiny black leather shoes on her boney feet. I sit on the treadle of the Singer sewing machine watching the woman as she talks to Mam, who's sitting as usual on her music stool. Our Bridd sitting on the easy chair by the fireplace with Eirwen on her knee, sits opposite the woman, who is perched on the horsehair sofa. Our Aderyn is back in the kitchen stirring stew on the fire. Our Dee is standing in the doorway between the front room and the kitchen, like a bird ready for flight.

Anyway, it goes like this. Being a good scholar like our Bram, Dee has passed the school leaving certificate early. But she's no use to our Mam in the house, as Mam keeps our Aderyn off school for all that stuff. Anyway, this woman explains about something called *Place*. She works in an office that finds *Places* for girls to work as servants, not just here in our town but all over the North. I remember a girl at school telling me her sister had gone to *Place* in Newcastle.

Now we all watch as the woman hands over a brown envelope to my mother. 'The *Place* is in Bradford,' she says. 'A village called Low Moor. The house is a boarding house. They need a good strong girl but they will train her up. There's a train ticket in the envelope and three shillings.' The envelope crackles in Mam's hand. The woman goes on. 'They will meet her off the train at Bradford station.'

The back door clashes as Dee storms out. The woman stands up and shakes hands with Mam, who wipes her hand down her pinny and then closes the front door after the woman.

Dee is furious all afternoon and stamps around the house like a giant. But Mam prevails and our Bram sits Dee down and talks her, his face close to here. So, the following Saturday all of us except Bram go to the station to see Dee onto the train. The platform is crowded and she looking smaller than usual the hat and coat she wears for chapel. No giant now.

After Dee has gone the house is very quiet. Too quiet for me. I can no longer hear her clattering around in her boots, or her shouting from the yard to some passing lads. This makes me very sad.

One day I come in from school to find a letter placed squarely in the middle of the kitchen table, just by the breadboard. I recognise our Dee's beautiful, sloping writing. But this letter is addressed to me, not our Mam, who pushes it across to me a scowl on her smooth white brow. 'Read it!' she says.

As I read the lines out loud I can hear my sister's voice.

Dear Ayla,

Well, here I am in <u>Place</u>*! The Missis met me off the train. We caught a bus which wound its way through a whole puzzle of streets, some of them with houses but some of them lined with buildings big as castles with chimneys like towers billowing bitter smoke which smells of burning iron. No elegant pit wheels here, Ayla! No sweet smell of coal.*

From the bus stop the Missis and me walked to the house together. This is a tall house in a row of much smaller narrower houses.

I am sharing a room and bed at the very top of the house with Myra Wilkes. She's the maid who will be my boss in this house. She's a fat lass with round cheeks and no neck. The Missis tells me I have to do everything Myra Wilkes says. My job is to work from seven in the morning to nine at night cleaning windows and scrubbing floors, possing clothes and swilling piss pails down the drains. This is from Monday morning to Saturday morning. On Saturday afternoon I walk into Bradford with Myra Wilkes and do the shopping for the Missis.

As I read our Dee's words I glance around the kitchen. The fire is roaring up the chimney and the water in the boiler beside it is bubbling. The big table is laid for the regular Wednesday baking which mostly our Aderyn does now. Even while I read Aderyn is busy tying on her blue apron. Our Evan is sitting on the treadle of the Singer sewing machine, his hands as usual whittling a stick. Our Breedlen and Eirwen are sitting on the fender. I lift the letter and look closely at the wall of writing before me – our Dee's pretty looping pretty words flow on line after line.

'Go on!' says Mam grimly.

I clear my throat and frown at the top sheet. *This is a lodging house.*

Two beds and five bedrooms. So you can imagine the washing and ironing with five lodgers to cater for. They are all men who work in the ironworks which are everywhere here, spewing smoke and making the day into night except for Sundays when the smoke thins out a bit. The Missis took my boots off me the day I arrived and shoved them in a cupboard under the stairs. (I found out later that she had sold them!) She brought me a pair of black shoes that still have the creases from the last wearer. But, like the missis says, the soles are good.

It's old and young men who board here and talk in all kinds of lingo. One man tried pinching my bottom. I told him off and punched his hand away. And the Missis gave me a right telling off for the setting up my cheek to one of her lodgers. Like I say they all talk funny here. Some sound Scottish, like our Angus grandma. Some have a funny twang, all whiny and in their jaws. Myra says they are from London. There are even foreigners here, from Italy and Poland. They are taller and more polite. One of them bowed to me!

I will stop now as my hand is aching. All I can tell you is that this place is worse than school. Much worse. Say hello to our Bram and Even and our lasses and to our Mam. Oh, now the Missis is shouting for me. Your sister Dee

PS I will not be here, long, Ayla. There's plenty of jobs for girls in Bradford in the mills and the shops. . That's what this Myra says – the one that I share a bed with.

PS 2. This whole town STINKS! Not the nice clean smell of coal but the perpetual smell of iron burning. It gets in your eyes and ears and soaks into your skin. In the end you don't notice it and you realise it is soaked into you and your inside and you have become the smell itself.

PS 3. I know that our Mam and our Chilton Granda will think that I've fallen into ungodly ways but the best thing about being here's going with the Missis to *what they call the Spiritualist Church. The Missis makes us go but when I finally get there I don't mind. The very first time I went, this old man took me on one side and told me that I had The Gift and gave me a shilling. Think of that! A.*

Dee's letters keep coming for five years, by which time she has her own boarding-house in Bradford as well as a husband, a stepson and five lodgers of her own. I keep all of her letters safe under my bed in her old schoolbag. And in time I will go to Bradford and live with her in her boarding-house and work in a woollen mill.

But that's another story.

1922. March 17. First birth control clinic set up in London.

ADERYN

1922. April 15 at the last minute railway and transport workers decide not to come out in support of the miners in this dispute with the coal owners.

My second sister is called Aderyn, which means *bird* in Welsh. But around here most people call her Ada, which to my mind means nothing really. So I call her Aderyn.

There's no denying our Aderyn is pretty. And, like our Mam and everyone in this family except me, she has this shiny black hair. Her eyes are blue and her skin, throughout the seasons, is a kind of dense white like fresh bread.

Aderyn is very modest and shy but I can see that the boys really like her: one in particular is Robbie Salter, the son of the grocer Albert Salter, whose family are regulars at our own chapel. Albert Salter fought in France alongside our Da. His Robbie doesn't work at the pit like most lads round here, so he doesn't have the ground-in grit and black rimmed eyes that are common among the pit lads. He has brown eyes and curly blonde hair and the deceptive face of an angel.

He hangs around with some lads outside the chapel to watch the people coming out. They call out to the girls and most girls call back before turning away to laugh with each other. Robbie runs to catch up with Aderyn and her best friend May, calling, 'Now, Ada!' Then he gets between them and joins them as they walk. The three of them stand at our back gate talking and laughing for a few minutes before Mam shouts, 'Get

16

yourself in here, Aderyn. There's work to do.'

Aderyn runs into the house to help Mam get on with the Sunday dinner. Our Bram loves Aderyn's Yorkshire puddings and relishes the way she does the vegetables from Mr Hunter's allotment. This makes it a special meal even if the meat is only a bit of rabbit or the scrag end of beef dropped off by the butcher who was also in France with our Da and doesn't forget it.

These days, being so useful to Mam in the house, Aderyn rarely goes to school, although she reads and writes well enough and knows her figures.

Every day has its task. Mondays washing, Tuesdays drying and ironing, Thursdays cleaning. Wednesdays and Fridays are baking days. On those days our Aderyn is at Mam's shoulder helping to knead the bread and bake the pies and cakes that keep us all going through the week. Our Eirwen and I are sometimes kept off school, pulled into helping with the kneading of the dough. But they never call on our Dee, whose hands are always too dirty.

It's because of the flour that Robbie knows Aderyn better than the other lads. They get together on Mondays and Thursdays when he walks with her from his father's shop, carrying the canvas sack containing a stone of flour, a weekly gift from his father: a gesture from an ex-soldier to the widow of his fallen comrade. When Robbie and Aderyn get to Wharfdale Street she takes the sack from him and clutches it to her like as baby. The truth is the lifesaving goodwill of his father means that our Mam doesn't mind so much about Robbie Salter being friendly with our

Aderyn.

As well as the Wednesday and Thursday baking days, Monday and Thursdays are bread days. Bread is a big thing in our house and in many of the houses in this town. Without it many families like ours would go hungry. The bread in our house takes us through the week for breakfasts, dinners and teas and fills Bram's tin bait-box (made by my Chilton Granda) for his dinner when he does his shift at the pit.   (I don't know why they call it a *bait* box. It's maybe down to the fact that in the olden days the men were fishermen as well as minors. And the fish-bait somehow becomes a man's bait in his bait tin.)

Wednesday and Saturday mornings are cake and pie days. I love seeing our Aderyn's small hands lifting the flour like a magician and watch it float back like snow into the big brown and cream baking bowl I'm at school on Wednesday but on Saturday I can sit and watch Aderyn about her flour magic. Her hands lift in the air and the flour falls like snowflakes in the air.

I especially like it when Aderyn makes Fairy Cakes. They are for a Sunday teatime, the only meal we have in the Front Room. Aderyn sets up a folding table in the middle of the room and we surround it with the chairs from the kitchen. Bram has pride of place on his seat in front of the fire especially lit for a good Sunday. Before our Dee goes to Bradford our Dee sits beside him.

Now for the Fairy Cakes. Aderyn has mixed flour and butter and sugar, and put the mixture in bun tin in the kitchen oven. The heat from the oven makes the buns rise like a range of little hills. Aderyn cut the top of the hill and splits them into two wings that she plants these on the pat of butter-cream she has placed on the top of the cakes.

There you have it. Butterfly cakes. Delicious.

Our Aderyn will get to marry Robbie Salter and will live in the next village in a house owned by his father, who has a few street houses down there. But that will be after she has had this baby called Billy. Our Mam is mad about this even when they later get married in the chapel. She says Aderyn and Robbie are too young to take care of the baby so Billy stays with us in Wharfedale Street and becomes our youngest brother. Our Evan is quite pleased as now he is no longer the youngest. He has a brother. He can stand tall.

Aderyn still comes home on Wednesdays and Fridays to do the baking but now I am roped in to help with the house doing Aderyn's chores. My life begins to tumble down.

In time Aderyn and Robbie will have another baby another boy, called Charlie, who stays with them in their little village house and grows into a more ordinary child, not like Billy. Billy will learn how to fly aeroplanes and will become a hero in the next war and, like our own Da, will die for his country. And I will visit the house in the bombed city where Robbie works on cars and our Aderyn always makes Fairy cakes on Saturdays.

1922. July 21. Navy shocked as planes sink ships.

BREEDLEN

19 October 1922 Prime Minister David Lloyd George resigns as his wartime coalition breaks up

My third sister's real name is Breedlen which means 'the helpful one'. Some folks still call her Breedlen but I call her Bridd. Some folks think her name is short for Bridget, which is an Irish name. But that's not right in this family. The only countries that we come from are Wales and Scotland.

But I do like to use her real name sometimes. *Breedlen!* It has a lovely sound. Mam calls her Breedlen too, now and then, but only when for some reason she's mad at her. But that's unusual, because Bridd is quiet, really good, and helpful in all kinds of practical ways. And she has the kindest, gentlest smile.

Bridd is shorter and squarer than our Aderyn, although she shares our sister's white skin and black hair. She is not pretty, but her face is as open and appealing as a flower. And she is just as quiet as our Dee is noisy. She turns out to be even more of a 'helpful one' when our Aderyn eventually has a baby, gets married and goes off to live in a nearby village. And so it is Bridd's turn to become our Mam's right-hand woman in Wharfdale Street. There is a big difference, but. Our Bridd is not the baker our Aderyn is, so Aderyn returns to Wharfdale Street on a Wednesday to bake cakes and a Saturday to bake pies.

But our Bridd is better than all of us at making things. She uses her pennies to buy discarded clothes at the Chapel jumble sales and cuts and converts dresses into skirts and blouses for our Eirwen and me and even shirts and short trousers for our Evan. She does her cutting out on the big kitchen table (where Aderyn weaves her cake-magic) and sits at the Singer sewing machine working through into the night, her feet beating a grinding rhythm as she pumps the treadle like mad.

As well as this, she unravels discarded jumpers from the jumble sales and winds the crinkled wool into skeins between her elbow and her thumb, then washes the skeins and hangs them on the line in the yard.

Our Bridd never uses patterns for the jumpers or the clothes. The patterns she uses must be in her head. The jumpers always fit and are a wonder of elaborate stitches. My favourite is the fine purple and green one that I still keep in a box under my bed with my books.

That can't happen, of course, if it's a washing day.

There will come a time when Bridd crochets her grand-daughter's wedding dress in two-ply wool. The bride will choose a modern lace concoction and the crocheted dress will never be worn and will remain sealed for many years in a suitcase on top of Bridd's wardrobe.

Like I say, our Bridd is a quiet person. She doesn't row with our Mam like Dee. In fact she's something of a ghostlike presence in the house. But she has this friend, a girl called Clarrie, whose brothers came up from Cornwall to work in the mines and harvest our coal.

21

There are two of them - Christopher and Paul. They have this allotment where they grow great prizewinning leeks and in the season Bridd and her friend Clarrie help them with their harvest. Bridd brings back potatoes and carrots, as well as leeks, to Wharfedale Street.

In time our Bridd gets on really well with Christopher, the big noisy brother, who is a hewer in the pit. We know from Bram that the hewers are the princes of the working men in the pit. Bridd says Christopher has told her that Cornwall is its own country, like Scotland and Wales. His brother Paul can sing songs in their own language.

In time Bridd will have to go off to Scarborough to work at a *place*, which is a big house on the promenade. One Saturday, though, Christopher will travel on the train and the bus to bring her back home. He turns up in Scarborough and drags her off the beach, where she goes for a Sunday walk with the housekeeper of the *place*. Eventually Christopher will marry our Breedlen and after that we don't see much of her. Christopher rules her life; he makes sure he fills her world. These Cornishman are all-engulfing, like the forward movement of the River Wear as it flows towards the sea.

Our family will shrink and there will be less work for those remaining in the house in Wharfdale Street. In the end everybody leaves. Even me, when I go off to the nurses' school in Harrogate.

But that's yet another story.

23 January 1924
Ramsay Macdonald becomes the first Labour prime minister

AYLA

*1924. In Italy Mussolini's Fascists achieve
a sweeping victory in the Italian General Election.*

You'll be wondering now about me. Me? I'm the third girl in this family of seven, and the fourth child. Sometimes this seems to make me invisible. To be honest it's a good place for a beady-eyed storyteller. After me come Eirwen and Evan who, being the little'ns, get quite a bit of petting and attention from the others.

I have to say that, like our Bram, I'm a good scholar. In fact I could read even *before* I went to school. Mebbe that started when our Aderyn helped me pick out words in the Book of Common Prayer while we waited for her cakes to rise. Then the time comes when our Bram insists to Mam that I should stay at school right until I'm fourteen. 'Might look to you like our Ayla's marking time, Ma. But she'll still go on learnin' new things, I'm tellen yer.'

And our Bridd brings me storybooks from her jumble sales – they only costs pennies and sometimes they're even given away. I have quite a collection of them now, under my bed. Some of them I read over and over again. I particularly like the poetry books because the words zing and stay in my head. I suppose all this means I do very well at school. So well, in fact, that Mrs Mason - one of my teachers - even invites me to her house for tea to play with her daughter, who goes to a different school but doesn't read as well as me. And Mrs Mason gives me books that are too battered to sit on the smart polished shelves in her house, which has a water toilet down the yard instead of a *nettie*. I sometimes make an excuse to go there, so I can sit for a while and then pull the chain to flush the water away. The walls of the toilet are painted green but there is no *boody* there. I'll tell you about *boody* in a minute,

The day after my tenth birthday Dee shows me the swearing game. To understand this you need to know that across the lane behind our houses there is this row of smallish buildings like large rabbit hutches. People-hutches I suppose. Dee's private name for them is *shithouses*, although our Bridd calls them *netties* and our Mam says their proper name is *earth closets*.

Anyway, this day I'm sitting on the back wall of our yard watching Dee make her way towards the Green to join her lad-gang. But she doesn't find them. She comes back and grabs my shoulder. 'Well, Ayla, pet, I bet you're dying to know the swearing game!'

I jump off the wall. 'Swearing game? What's that?' My voice is squeaking with excitement. There's always excitement around our Dee.

She clutches my arm and leads me to the back wall of our own *nettie*. Or *earth closet*. Or *shithouse* - whatever you call it. My Mam says these people-hutches are away from the house because of the smell. To be honest I don't really notice the smell - either outside or inside the *nettie*. I suppose you get used to it. Sometimes I notice people who bring the smell away with them. But, funnily enough, nobody in our house seems to. Or maybe we're just used to each other.

Dee drags me to the back wall of the *nettie*. She stands before me and says, 'Now, Ayla! Get hold of the back of your skirt!' She puts her hand through her legs and pulls the back hem of her skirt before tucking it into the leather belt at her waist. She stands there, looking like some Eastern prince wearing pantaloons. I blink at her, thinking that she's like a picture in one of the storybooks that I got off Mrs Mason. I put my hand through my own legs haul out my own hem to tuck it into the waistband of the skirt that Bridd made for me for my birthday, out of one of Dee's Sunday dresses.

Now I watch Dee as she bends over and puts both hands on the packed-earth ground and flings her boots up against the wall. Now she is entirely upside down, her hair falling down over her face. She shakes her head, looks up at me and speaks with her jumper almost covering your mouth. 'Come on!' she says. 'Your turn, Ayla.'

I place my hands on the hard earth and fling my legs up against the wall. It's not that hard.

'Now, swear!' She commands.

'What?' My mouth, like hers, is muffled by my jumper.

'Swear!' she orders. 'When you're upside down you can swear, Ayla! God canna hear you swearing when you're upside down.' Now her voice deepens until it's almost like a boy's voice. 'Bloody-bugger-bloody-bugger-bloody bugger.' She takes a deep breath. 'Now swear, Ayla!' She shouts at the top of her voice.

I'm upside down, so - funnily enough - I don't feel shocked. So I swear. 'Bloody-bugger-bloody-bugger!'

'Louder!' she commands. 'Louder Ayla!'

So I swear louder. And I swear more. And somehow it's really wonderful. My head is buzzing.

Then there is a clatter as she drops back onto her booted feet and I follow suit with less of a clatter. 'See!' she says, 'Every time you are sick and tired of your life and the folks around you are getting inside your head, you can get up on your hands against the wall and swear your head off. Feels good doesn't it?'

Suddenly the air is filling with loud yells and we both turn to see the lads on the other side of the Green. It's Dee's lad-gang galloping towards us, shouting and pushing at each other. One lad is riding on the back of another, riding him like he's a horse.

I just stand there. In no time Dee is racing away and the lads are chasing after her. I feel good. She's right. You do feel better after swearing upside down. These days I do it even when she's not there. When it's raining I do it against the wash-house wall with the door shut. Like I say, she's right. It does make you feel better when you're sick and tired and things. And of people.

When I'm sick and tired of people I sometimes go out and sit on the *nettie* – sorry *earth closet* – even when I don't need to *go*. It's the one place in the house where I can be on my own. I like to stare up at the *boody,* glistening in jam jars on the shelf above the door. If you don't know what boody is, it's the treasures that you find all around you - things like broken marbles, bright pebbles or brass buttons, seashells or dead flowers. Anything that catches the light. They glow through the glass of the jam jar like stars. That's why they're called *boody* - a baby name for beautiful things. When I sit there and stare at the *boody* jars I kind of calm down and forget to cry.

I sometimes wonder if Dee still goes upside down against a wall to swear when she's in Bradford or if there's something else that calms her down. Not that she cries. Dee never cries.

When I'm 14 I too will go into *place* like our Dee and Aderyn – not away, but at a doctor's house near the High Street in our own town. But I only last a week there before the doctor's wife gives me the sack for quoting the poet Longfellow, telling me I am lazy. 'You are just standing there dreaming, instead of mopping the floor!' The doctor's wife tells Mam I am 'not suitable for domestic work'. That's when our Bram suggests to Mam that I should go to Bradford to live with our Dee and get work in in a woollen mill. That's no punishment, to be honest.

In Bradford, one of Dee's lodgers is a male nurse in the local mental hospital. I love his tales of the wards and the strange people. In the end he tells me about this college in Harrogate where even if you are a girl you can train to be a nurse.

To be honest, I sometimes wonder whether you find your fate or it's your fate that finds you.

September18. Mahatma Ghandi on hunger strike in despair at the recent riots between Hindus and Moslem

EIRWEN

'It came upon the midnight clear…'

Our Bridd and me are coming down the yard in the crisp spring sunshine when we hear Eirwen's sweet voice piercing the air. Sounds like she's practising her hymns with our Mam. We peer through the kitchen window to find Eirwen and Mam are not on their own. Two men are sitting at the kitchen table with Mam; Eirwen is standing beside her singing her heart out. Breedlen and me lurk out in the scullery, listening to them talking. Breedlen whispers in my ear. 'The tall thin one is the Minister for our district, Mr Brocklehurst. And the fat one is Mr. Gale, the preacher that travels around. They're sorting out this year's Anniversary.'

'It came upon the midnight clear…'

In the kitchen Eirwen's voice fades.

Both men grunt their approval. Then there is a shuffling of papers and the deep voice of the Minister bells out into the scullery. 'Aye, Mrs Angus, your bairn's got a fine voice. That'll do nicely for the Anniversary. We can fit it in here in the order of service.' More rustling. He goes on, 'room for another one. Has she got another one Mrs Angus?'

Now Eirwen's voice pierces the space again right into the scullery, *'Let all the world in every corner sing.'*

Mr Gale speaks. 'Very nice, Mrs Angus, very nice.' And then there is more rustling as Mam shepherds the men through the middle door, through the front room and out of the door.

Now Breedlen and me can go into the kitchen and join Mam and Eirwen, who grins across. 'Ayla! I'm gonna sing two songs at the Anniversary she says. 'Me!'

For a second I want to smack her. She's so pleased with herself. The truth is she's our Mam's favourite even though she does nothing for the house - except the singing, which comes naturally.

Me? I'm feeling more invisible today. And I don't like it. So I turn and run out of the house and go up on my hands against to the Nettie wall and swear my heart out to stop myself crying.

The highlight of our chapel year is always the Anniversary. It happens some time in May, to celebrate the births of John and Charles Wesley, the two brothers who started up the whole chapel thing more than two hundred years ago. According to our Bram they did that to fight against slavery and escape what he calls the iron hand of the Church of England.

These celebrations involve sermons, songs and poems followed by sandwiches, cakes and big pots of tea. All the children learn 'pieces' - poems and passages learnt by heart - and stand at the front to recite them. Of course our Eirwen sings her songs. The women, including Mam and our Aderyn, bake for three days and fill special baskets to take along for the Anniversary tea.

Our Anniversary is on a different Sunday to the one in the Chilton chapel, so Mam can play the organ at both the celebrations. Our Eirwen sings at Chilton too. She even knows some songs in Welsh. But the rest of us don't go there to say our pieces, because we don't speak Welsh.

As well as the pieces from the children, there is a sermon and wild preaching from My Gale, and people from the congregation reading out from the John Wesley's sermons and passages from the Bible that are so strong they can make you shiver. Then there are the songs and the children's pieces that don't have to be from the Bible or even the Book of Common Prayer. But they have to be about being good and doing the right thing.

Everyone dresses up in best clothes and I feel proud of my sisters for looking so smart. Even Evan has brushed back his black curls and wears a tie that is borrowed from Bram, who is very smart himself in the clothes he used to wear when he worked at the tailor's in the high street. They are quite tight now but far cry from his pit clothes.

Me, I only ever choose poetry for my piece. At one Anniversary I recite some verses from Alfred Lord Tennyson which earn a blank silence rather than the prickle of approval that greets Eirwen's songs. Our Bridd muttered to me afterwards, 'A bit heavy going, Ayla, but you say the words very nicely.'

Oh! Our Eirwen can certainly sing, She's been singing since she was a baby, sitting beside our Mam at the harmonium. At first she would hum without words as she sat there. I once heard our Mam say to a neighbour, 'No denying the bairn has the gift. She's pitch-perfect on every note.' It's such a rare thing for Mam to actually boast about any of us. Except Bram of course.

When Eirwen sings her solos there are murmurs of appreciation in the congregation but no applause. At the end of every spoken piece there is a prickle of approval from the crowded chapel but no applause. That's not allowed.

The fact is that singing is our Eirwen's only thing. She was very slow to learn to read and is hopeless at arithmetic. Our Aderyn couldn't teach her to bake and our Breedlen couldn't teach her to sew. But she gets away with all this in our Mam's eyes, because she 'sings like an angel'. Anniversaries, I suppose, are the place where angels get to shine.

And handwriting is certainly not Eirwen's thing. It looks like a spider has been travelling across the page. Mam has spent a lot of time showing her how to write and how to hold the pen. The trouble is Eirwen is clumsy and her writing is ugly. Mam's own writing, like our Dee's, is very fine and flowing - and much admired. Our Dee told me once that that in the Great War Mam used to write love letters for her sisters-in-law and the wives of my dad's brothers who fought alongside him in France.

But Mam never spoke of that to me.

As you would expect, our Eirwen doesn't like school, and more than once gets the cane for not listening to the teacher. But she makes a friend at school, called Meg Styles - an ugly, flat-faced, bossy girl who follows Eirwen home and often sits at our table like she's one of us. Coming from East Durham, she has a very strong accent, and speaks strangely, through the side of her mouth. She even sits on the other side of Mam when she's practising the harmonium. Mam doesn't seem to mind and gives Meg pies and cakes to take home because her dad has run off and her Mam is always poorly.

One day at school Eirwen and Meg get into bother when they run out of the playground and go down to the woods. After school Eirwen brings a note home from the teacher and hands it to Mam, who sends her to bed early for three nights as punishment.

(I say one thing for our Mam. She never hits you, like Meg's Mam does. Still, one bad look from our Mam is like a belt across your back. Our Aderyn told me that Meg *did* get the belt from her mother, who wasn't too poorly for that.)

I never say it but I secretly think our Eirwen is spoiled and can get away with most things. But even I admire her at the Anniversary, when her voice rises to the rafters and sends a shiver down my spine.

Post Scriptum

As time goes on Eirwen will pursue her gift for choosing bad friends, including a husband who runs away after three years, leaving her and Mam with two ginger-haired boys to raise. Then it happens that, working in an armaments factory, Eirwen will meet and become close friends with a bossy woman called Enid - a person not unlike Meg Styles. The terrible thing is that when our Mam eventually dies this Enid will move into the house in Wharfdale Street and take charge of the household along with her pitman husband, who is also

32

a Methodist preacher and travels round the villages to preach in market places and chapels, persuading people to love Jesus. Luckily I don't have to suffer any of this because, by then, I will be living away and going out with an electrician who works in in the mental hospital where I am a nurse.

Eventually our Eirwen will sing at my wedding in the Wesleyan Chapel where she used to sing and where we said our pieces at the Anniversaries. As I stand there, having made my vows, Eirwen   sings her heart out, and her voice - now a confident contralto - rises above the congregation, filling the chapel with a sense of celebration which quite equals that at every Anniversary.

Dec 6. 1926. The first Impressionist artist Claude Monet dies at his home in Giverny in Normandy,

EVAN

1930. April 21 Amy Johnson, the 27-year-old daughter of a wholesale fish-merchant, arrived today in Darwin, the first woman to fly from Britain to Australia solo.

The first time my eldest brother Bram calls Mam, 'Ma', is when Evan, my youngest brother, is in trouble.

I can see it now: Evan is standing there like a shorn sheep at harvest time, my sister Breedlen standing beside him, with her arms folded and her big dressmaking scissors in the crook of her arm. Around Evan's feet is a heap of the black curls that have been his crowning glory since he was born.

Breedlen holds up the scissors and mutters, 'These'll be blunt now. What good will they be for cutting my cloth?'

'Dinnet be worried about that, Bridd,' says Bram, who has just walked into the room. 'I'll take our Evan down to Joe Coggins and our Evan can ask him very nicely if he'll sharpen them for you in between shoeing the horses.' He punches Evan on the shoulder. 'Won't you Evan?'

Jo Coggins is the pit blacksmith who does some tool work in his shed for some of the tradesmen. He is a big man shoulders like cliff edges.

Now Evan's shorn head is moving up and down like a nodding doll as he avoids Breedlen's glare.

'They'll be as good as new, Bridd.' Bram assures her. 'You can count on that.' It's Breedlen's turn to nod. She hands over the scissors. We all usually agree with Bram. He's pretty wise. And he's the oldest after all.

Our Evan's lucky that Bram's not mad at him. These days Evan has stopped helping Bram with his after-shift bath. This started one day when Mam shouted Evan in from the back street to help with Bram's bath. He wriggles in Breedlen's grip and glowers at Mam. 'I'm sick of it Mam. I get all black too,' he says. 'And there's blood.'

Mam's face darkens at that and she thrusts Evan out of the house. Our Bridd and me offer to do the job but Mam shakes her head, saying, 'They're the only boys in the house of women. Wouldn't be right for any of you to do it. I bathed him naked as a bairn so now it's down to me again.' After that Mam's takes over the job of washing the coal dust from Bram's back and bathing the blood and blue bruises where his back has scraped the low seams underground.

To be honest, all of us have a very warm spot for our Evan It's true that – like our Eirwen - he's a bit spoilt. But he's a boy and is the youngest so he mostly gets away with it. All of us pay him a lot of attention. I read to him and tell him stories. Our Aderyn makes him special pies and cakes. Our Bridd makes all his clothes, until he goes to school. Our Bram canters down the back lane with him on his shoulders.

As Evan gets older he gets naughtier. He starts to get lost at mealtimes – a thing that the rest of us never risk, to avoid Mam's wrath. He runs away from Breedlen when she chases after him to bring him in for his tea. But Evan is quickly forgiven and is given his dinner or tea, set is a special place on the empty table.

Oh yes, we all get mad at him! Our Dee shouts at him when Mam's not there. Our Eirwen pinches him and makes him cry. Of course this stops when he is old enough to tell Mam who did it with a tear in his eye.

As he grows taller he learns to enjoy the rough-and-tumble of the playground and the back lane. In time he gathers a gaggle of boys around him and they roam the back lane, throwing sticks and bricks into the backyards when they think nobody is looking.

Underneath all this is the fact that Evan is brighter than our Eirwen and as bright as the rest of us, even Bram. He quite likes school and is quick to learn. Being especially fond of our Bram, he likes to be near him when he's in the house. On Sundays and weeknights, when he's not the pit, Mam allows Bram to spend time in the front room, excluding himself from this house of women, buried in books that he has borrowed from a man at the Union. Spread all around him on the front room carpet, these books tell the story in words and pictures of the underground world of the pit.

Evan sometimes sneaks in and sits beside Bram, not speaking, but peering at the pages with their colourful maps showing the veins underground - things our Bram calls *strata*. I know this because I stand at the middle door listening. I hear Bram telling Evan, 'This is the wealth of our county Evan, under our very feet, see? Our gift of wealth to the whole country. You should know, son, that without the skills and the work of the Durham pitmen, no man and no country will ever see this wealth or feel the benefit.'

So our Evan doesn't follow Bram into the pit. When he leaves school Bram fixes him up with an apprenticeship with Mr Coggins, the pit blacksmith who sharpened Breedlen's scissors. But working with Mr Coggins Evan is not confined to sharpening scissors or shoeing horses. He learns to mend metal things fasten bits of shoot machinery that are broken down. He has to pip up meagre pay from Jo Coggins to our Mam but she does give him some pocket money. He saves this up to buy the smart clothes that he wears on Saturday nights strolling the High Street with his friends. Our Bridd calls him quite the dandy with his narrow trousers and his royal blue neckerchief.

One day Mr Coggins' brother comes up from Birmingham where he is a foreman in a car factory. He leans against the wall in Mr Coggins workshop and watches Evan work on a broken clock. Later, talking to our Bram he says he'd like to take Evan back to Birmingham. 'He's a talented lad.'

Our Mam will object and our Bram will support her but Mr Coggins has a word with Bram who changes his mind, telling Evan that he should try his luck in Birmingham, where Mr Coggins has promised to fix him up with an apprenticeship to a toolmaker

. 'It's a big city, Evan,' says Bram. 'New things are happening there. Good chances for a clever lad like you.' He looks at Mam, 'Isn't that so, Ma?' So our Mam is finally persuaded to agree. She even buys Evan a suitcase to take on the train. We all gather at the station to say goodbye to him but none of us cry. We are our mother's daughters, after all.

Our Bram hears from Mr Coggins that very soon Evan has won praise from his toolmaker boss for his inventive skill with mechanical things and, it seems, is even popular with his fellow toolmakers. We hear about this from his postcards and very short letters.

But in truth Evan will just about vanish from our lives. He turns up now and then with a present for Mam and a book for Bram. Each time he turns up he seems taller and more grown up. His thick black hair is now slicked back with oil and his clothes get more and more fancy. And we will notice that his way of speaking changes. He doesn't sound like he comes from here anymore. His voice is all in his jaw and his words rap out like bullets. In truth, all our ways of speaking are changing. Me with my hospital talk, Dee with her Bradford accent, our Bridd with the Cornish tones she picks up from Christopher.

Each time Evan turns up at the house in Wharfdale Street his clothes get better and fancier. His thick black hair is now swept back from his broad, wide forehead. Then he starts wearing a trilby instead of a cap and a bright tie, big collared shirt and a black woollen overcoat. He draws glances all along the High Street and all down the lane behind Wharfedale Street.

'Looks like a tally man, our Evan, out tocollect his money,' says our Breedlen.   .

March 10. 1930. Unemployment in Britain
tops 1.5 million

SIBLINGS

POST SCRIPTUM

2022

So, here you have our time. With the spirit of our Mam at our shoulders, we seven siblings will grow up through the 20th century. Our Bram will be the big man at the pit and our Evan will be the big man in his car factory. And the rest of us – all girls with our various gifts, skills and talents - will make our mark with our families, in our home life. Of the girls, only our Eirwen and I will add to this home life our experience in, and absorb the language of, hospitals factories and prisons. So this is our century.

1938. Chamberlain flies home and promises 'peace for our time'.

SOME OTHER WR PUBLICATIONS

Kaleidoscope – Short Story Collection
With Such Caution – Prose Poems
The Bad Child – Family Politics
An Englishwoman in France - Contemporary
No Rest for the Wicked - Theatrical History
Cruelty Games - Crime
The Lavender House   - London
Journey to Moscow - Contemporary History
Family Ties – Family Politics
Sandie Shaw and The Millionth Marvell Cooker - Factory life.
The Woman Who Drew Buildings - Poland in 1981
Riches of The Earth - 20th Century Trilogy
Under a Brighter Sky - Migrating from Ireland.
Land of Your Possession - Aftermath of the Coventry Blitz.
A Dark Light Shining - 1930s Girl travels to France)
Honesty's Daughter -1905. Young woman goes the America.
A Woman Scorned - The Story of Mary Ann Cotton
Kitty Rainbow – (1) First of a Trilogy
Children of the Storm - (2) WW1
A Thirsting Land   - (3) Post War Britain
Pauley's Web, - Prison life
The Bad - (3) Post WW2)
The Jagged Window - Mid Twentieth Century
Gabriel Painting - An original 'pitman painter
My Dark Eyed Girl - Spanish Civil War
The Long Journey Home - WW2 Internment in Singapore)
The Pathfinder – 400 AD. Celts vs Romans)

CHILDREN'S NOVELS

Theft
Lizza
The Real Life of Studs McGuire

Printed in Great Britain
by Amazon

80147771R00032